mel bay presents
The Student Violist:
Handel
by Craig Duncan

Visit us on the Web at http://www.melbay.com — E-mail us at email@melbay.com

Contents

This collection of Handel's music comes from his sonatas, orchestral works and incidental pieces. The selections are on an easy grade level, playable in first position. The book begins with the easiest arrangements and progresses in level of difficulty. Most of the piano parts double the viola to aid in performance.

Menuet
from The Royal Fireworks

George Frederic Handel

Bourrée
from the Water Music Suite II in D

George Frederic Handel

Passepied

George Frederic Handel

Rigaudon

George Frederic Handel

Gavotte in C
from Opus 5 Number 2

George Frederic Handel

March
from Opus 5 Number 2

George Frederic Handel

Gavotte
from Opus 5 Number 1

George Frederic Handel

Balli

from Alceste

George Frederic Handel

mel bay presents
The Student Violist:
Handel
by Craig Duncan

Contents

This collection of Handel's music comes from his sonatas, orchestral works and incidental pieces. The selections are on an easy grade level, playable in first position. The book begins with the easiest arrangements and progresses in level of difficulty. Most of the piano parts double the viola to aid in performance.

Menuet
from The Royal Fireworks

George Frederic Handel

Bourrée
from the Water Music Suite II in D

George Frederic Handel

Passepied

George Frederic Handel

Rigaudon

George Frederic Handel

Gavotte in C

from Opus 5 Number 2

George Frederic Handel

March
from Opus 5 Number 2

George Frederic Handel

Gavotte
from Opus 5 Number 1

George Frederic Handel

Balli
from Alceste

George Frederic Handel

Aylesford March

George Frederic Handel

Royal Fireworks Theme

from the Overture

George Frederic Handel

Menuett
from Opus 5 Number 4

George Frederic Handel

Allegro Moderato

Rondeau
from Opus 5 Number 3

George Frederic Handel

ritard

15

Aylesford March

George Frederic Handel

18

Royal Fireworks Theme

from the Overture

George Frederic Handel

Maestoso

Menuett
from Opus 5 Number 4

George Frederic Handel

Rondeau
from Opus 5 Number 3

George Frederic Handel

27

29